SPIRITUAL

VICTORY

JESSE L. NELSON

SPIRITUAL

VICTORY

HOW TO BE AN OVERCOMER

JESSE NELSON MINISTRIES

SPIRITUAL VICTORY:
HOW TO BE AN OVERCOMER
©2017 by Jesse L. Nelson

Published by Jesse Nelson Ministries

Unless otherwise noted "Scripture quotations taken from the New American Standard Bible®, Copyright © 1960, 1962, 1963, 1968, 1971, 1972, 1973, 1975, 1977, 1995 by The Lockman Foundation Used by permission." (www.Lockman.org)

Scripture quotations are taken from the Holy Bible, New Living Translation, copyright ©1996, 2004, 2007, 2013, 2015 by Tyndale House Foundation. Used by permission of Tyndale House Publishers, Inc., Carol Stream, Illinois 60188. All rights reserved.

Scripture quotations marked MSG are taken from *THE MESSAGE*, copyright © 1993, 1994, 1995, 1996, 2000, 2001, 2002 by Eugene H. Peterson. Used by permission of NavPress. All rights reserved. Represented by Tyndale House Publishers, Inc.

Printed in the United States of America

ISBN-10: 0-9971778-1-0
ISBN-13: 978-0-9971778-1-7

Cover by Catesha Nelson
contact: jacecatesha@mac.com

This project is dedicated to my mother,

Martha Ann Nelson.

She lived in spiritual victory from start to finish!

February 7, 1954-February 11, 2014

CONTENTS

INTRODUCTION

Do you know the keys to spiritual victory? As a pastor, I constantly encounter Christians that feel defeated. Many of them have similar emotional profiles. First, they consider themselves spiritual underdogs with no chance of winning in life. They have a negative aura oozing from their spirits. They are insecure about their relationship with God. They feel like they are always losing. They do not think the "best is yet to come" because they really believe the worst days are ahead. They feel hopeless, helpless, and trapped with no way out. These Christians need spiritual victory. What about you? Do you desire spiritual victory?

Emotional Profile for Defeated Christians
1. No chance of winning
2. Negative spirit
3. Insecure
4. Feel like a loser
5. No vision of future
6. Hopeless or helpless
7. Trapped

How do you feel when you think about spiritual victory in your life?

DO YOU FEEL...

CRUSHED? Like everything is pressing you down.

FRUSTRATED? Like nothing is in your favor.

STUMPED? Like you can't figure out what to do.

DISCOURAGED? Like nothing makes you happy.

DEPRESSED? Like you have no desire.

BLOCKED? Like something is always in your way.

CRIPPLED? Like you are broken.

BURDENED? Like you have too much to overcome.

DO YOU FEEL LIKE YOU NEED MORE OF SOMETHING?

Something DEEPER than you can reach?

Something GREATER than you can imagine?

Something BIGGER than life?

Do you feel like you have a hole in your spiritual bucket? To make matters worse, you see other Christians living in spiritual victory!

You see them living the Jesus life, an abundant life. Instead of being burdened, they are blessed.

They are not frustrated because God's favor flushes out their frustration. We are discouraged because we see them dominate the same things that defeat us. Then you begin to wonder, "what are they doing?" "Do they know a secret for spiritual victory?" However, we are too ashamed and prideful to ask those living in *victory* how to attain it because we should know how to live in *victory*. Right? We think spiritual victory comes as a result of doing everything right!

WE DO EVERYTHING RIGHT…

We go to church!

We read our Bibles!

We pray and fast!

We give our tithe and offering!

We serve in ministry!

AND WE STOPPED…

Sinning, cursing, drinking, clubbing, cheating, lusting, lying, stealing, gambling and coveting!

After all these changes we are still losing and getting further behind instead of moving ahead. We have questions about spiritual victory but no answers.

We turn to our friends, but they have no answers that really work! We watch various television programs, but the host talks more about our problems than solutions. We read books and blogs trying to discover the keys to spiritual victory.

Today we are going to do something different! We are going to search the Bible for our answer. I hope that this book will help you discover biblical keys for spiritual victory. Certainly, we cannot discover *all* the keys to spiritual victory in this brief study, but I believe we will have enough keys to become overcomers. Are you ready for a life of spiritual victory? Do you want to be an overcomer? Turn the page and begin to get the keys to your spiritual victory!

1

KNOW THE SECRET

What do you think is God's secret to spiritual victory? Initially, it seems odd to think that God has secrets. In a world where secrets are taboo, we reject the idea of God having secrets, but God has secrets. The Bible speaks of God's secrets. Here are a few references:

Deuteronomy 29:29 reads, "The secret things belong to the LORD our God, but the things revealed belong to us and to our sons forever, that we may observe all the words of this law."

Job 15:8 reads, "Do you hear the secret counsel of God, and limit wisdom to yourself?"

Psalms 28:14 reads, "The secret of the LORD is for those who fear Him, And He will make them know His covenant."

Romans 16:25 reads, "Now to Him who is able to establish you according to my gospel and the preaching of Jesus Christ, according to the revelation of the mystery which has been kept secret for long ages past."

God has secrets; however, God does not keep the keys to spiritual victory a secret. He reveals it to us through His word, the Bible.

Although there are many passages of scripture that have keys for spiritual victory, we are going to turn our attention to 1 John 5:4-5. These two verses give us three (3) keys to spiritual victory.

1 John 5:4-5 reads, "For whatever is born of God overcomes the world; and this is the victory that has overcome the world—our faith. Who is the one who overcomes the world, but he who believes that Jesus is the Son of God?" Did you see a key to victory? Let's read these verses in two other Bible translations for better clarity.

The New Living Translation reads, "For every child of God defeats this evil world, and we achieve this victory through our faith. And who can win this battle against the world? Only those who believe that Jesus is the Son of God"

The Message reads, "Every God-begotten person conquers the world's ways. The conquering power that brings the world to its knees is our faith.

The person who wins out over the world's ways is simply the one who believes Jesus is the Son of God."

So, what is one of the keys to victory? FAITH! What is faith? Hebrews 11:1 reads, "Faith is the substance of things hoped for and the evidence of things not seen." Here is my definition: "Faith is putting your hope and confidence in God and His word." When you have faith, you believe God will do something about your situation. Do you have faith? No faith, no victory…little faith, little victory…much faith, much victory! Simply put, you need faith for spiritual victory. Is faith really that important? Let's scan Hebrews 11, and see what people did *through* faith.

Hebrews 11 lists men and women from the Old Testament that demonstrated great faith in God.

One of my favorite men of faith is Noah. I know Abraham receives recognition for his faith in God, but Noah's faith was proven before Abraham's. Noah's story begins in Genesis 6.

In Genesis 6, God regretted making man and placing him on earth because he saw that men desired evil more than good. While grieving over the sinfulness of man, God noticed Noah and Noah "found favor in the eyes of the Lord." Noah was righteous, blameless, and walked faithfully with God. God told Noah of the plan to destroy humanity. Then God instructed Noah to build an ark, so that Noah could save his family, and other animals on the earth.

What did Noah do? He did not question God. He did not debate with God. He did not doubt God. Noah had faith in the word of God and obeyed the command of God. This means Noah began building the ark and gathering the food and animals.

It was approximately 70 years between God's initial conversation with Noah and the actual fulfillment of God's word. Can you imagine the questions people, especially the family, were asking Noah for 70 years?

"What are you building?"

"When are you going to finish?"

"When is the flood coming?"

"Are you sure God talked to you?"

I wonder what was Noah thinking while he was building the ark? Year after year, Noah's family and friends challenged his faith. How did Noah overcome the negativity he may have experienced? Noah's faith helped him finish building the ark in the face of adversity. Faith kept Noah faithful to God's command.

In Genesis 7, God returned to Noah and told him to prepare for entering the ark in seven days. I wonder what that the last week was like on earth? What were Noah's last words to his friends? How did Noah stay focused? How many people laughed at Noah? Noah had to persevere through this unknown territory by having faith in God. Noah did not see God's word was fulfilled until he heard the first drops of rain fall upon the ark. Noah teaches us that faith is not seeing but believing.

Noah was not the only person of faith in Hebrews 11. Through faith Abel offered a better sacrifice to God than Cain. Through faith Enoch did not see death but walked to heaven with God. Through faith Abraham followed God without knowing where he was going. Through faith Sarah was able to conceive a son at an old age. Through faith Abraham obeyed God and saved his son's life. Through faith Moses led the Israelites across the Red Sea to freedom from Egyptian slavery.

Through faith Rahab saved her family by helping God's men. Through faith many people lived in spiritual victory: Gideon, Barak, Samson, Jephthah, David, Samuel, Esther, Shadrack, Meshach, Abednigo, and all the prophets.

We see what they did through faith, but what about us? How does faith help us attain spiritual victory? Let's notice the details of 1 John 5:4 again, "For whatever is born of God overcomes the world; and this is the victory that has overcome the world—our faith."

Did you see what faith does for us? Faith is a key for spiritual victory! Faith makes us winners. Faith makes us overcomers. The word overcome comes from the Greek word "nike" which means more than just do it! Overcome means to conquer, to have victory, or to have superiority. Therefore, an overcomer has conquering power, victory, and superiority in their life.

Faith gives every child of God the power to overcome any situation and opponent. Because of faith we are able to overthrow our enemy so that everyone (the world) sees our victory. The word "overcome" does not indicate a struggle, but an overpowering dominance. The word "overcome" in the biblical context conveys the idea that the believer has continual victory over the world.[1]

Therefore, winning is a lifestyle. Christians should be walking, living, breathing, thinking, and talking victory. Faith gives us the victory. Faith gives us strength. What else does faith do for us?

Here are 30 facts from the New Testament about faith in the Christian's life.

Faith Facts

1. We are saved through faith (Eph. 2:8).
2. We understand creation through faith (Heb.11:3).
3. We please God through faith (Heb. 11:6).

4. We can move mountains through faith (Matt. 21:21).

5. We are purified through faith (Gal. 2:16).

6. We live by faith (Rom. 1:17).

7. We are tested because of our faith (James 1:3).

8. We walk by faith (2 Cor. 5:7).

9. We stand firm through faith (2 Cor. 1:24).

10. We are healed through faith (Luke 7:50; 8:3,4).

11. We are forgiven through faith (Luke 5:20).

12. We are cleaned through faith (Acts 15:9).

13. We are strengthened through faith (Acts 16:5).

14. We become sons and daughters of Abraham through faith (Gal. 3:7).

15. We become children of God through faith (Gal. 3:36).

16. We have ? boldness and confidence through faith (Eph. 3:12).

17. We have the patience to wait through faith (Gal. 5:5).

18. We build up ourselves through faith (Jude 1:20).

19. Christ dwells in our heart through faith (Eph. 3:17).

20. We accept others through faith (Rom 14:1).

21. We attain the power of God through faith (1 Cor. 2:5).

22. We love through faith (Eph. 6:23).

23. We are comforted through faith (1 Thess. 3:7).

24. We inherit the powers of God through faith (Heb. 6:12).

25. We persevere through faith (Rev. 14:12).

26. We pray through faith (James 1:6).

27. We receive the spirit through faith (Gal. 3:2).

28. We are shielded through faith (Eph. 6:17,18).

29. We are protected through faith (1 Peter 1:5).

30. We are resurrected through faith (Col. 2:12).

When was your last spiritual battle? Did you win or lose? Faith is the difference between spiritual victory and spiritual defeat. Faith was the difference when David killed Goliath. Faith was the difference when Daniel spent the night in the lion's den.

Faith was the difference for Shadrach, Meshach, and Abednego when they were thrown into the fiery furnace. Faith was the difference between their spiritual victory and spiritual defeat. If you want spiritual victory you need faith! Faith by itself is not enough to win. You must put your hope and confidence in God to be victorious. Keep reading and discover more keys to spiritual victory.

Think About It!

1. What is a key to victory?

2. What is faith?

3. How do you define faith?

4. What does faith do for us?

5. Who is an overcomer?

2

KNOW YOUR ENEMIES

You have enemies! I know that may be shocking news for you, but it is true. Everyone does not want you to live in spiritual victory. Your enemies want you to live a defeated life. Your enemies frown when they see you smile. They grin when something negative happens to you. They grit their teeth when you respond to negative circumstances with the positive affirmation that "God is good all the time, and all the time God is good." They dance when you fall. They never try to help you up.

You have real enemies! One of the keys to spiritual victory is knowing your enemies. So who is our enemy? I believe we have two type of enemies. One enemy is obvious and the other enemy is not so obvious. Let's discuss the *obvious* enemy first.

The obvious enemy is Satan. Who is Satan? Since the serpent persuaded Eve to eat the forbidden fruit in the garden of Eden, Satan has been a "thorn in the flesh" to all humanity. Satan is the chief of demons. Throughout the Bible we see him as the agitator of God. His name means adversary.[1]

According to Ezekiel 28:12-19, Satan was the model of perfection and full of wisdom. He was made of gold and precious stones like jasper and emerald. He was the "anointed cherub."

Satan guarded or covered the throne of God and had full access to the presence of God.

He was blameless until the day his pride became overwhelming, and he sinned against God.

Isaiah 14:12-17 teaches us about the rise and fall of Satan. The devil desired to elevate himself above God. We can see Satan's aspirations in his five (5) I will statements:

1. I will ascend to heaven.
2. I will place my throne above God's.
3. I will preside on the mountain.
4. I will climb above the clouds.
5. I will be like the Most High.

How did God respond to this rebellion? God said: "I will throw you into the pit of death and people will see you powerless and ask if you were the one causing all the trouble in the world." Satan's desire led to his destruction.

Since Satan cannot beat God, He is always trying to defeat us. He uses the same tricks today that he used yesterday.

What is Satan's strategy for defeating us?

1. **He tempts us to sin**. Satan never makes us sin, but he entices us with our own temptation. "Let no one say when he is tempted, "I am being tempted by God"; for God cannot be tempted by evil, and He Himself does not tempt anyone. But each one is tempted when he is carried away and enticed by his own lust" (James 1:13-14).

2. **He distracts us from God's priorities**. "But He turned and said to Peter, "Get behind Me, Satan! You are a stumbling block to Me; for you are not setting your mind on God's interests, but man's" (Matthew 16:23).[2]

3. **He snatches the word of God from us**. "Satan comes and takes away the word which has been sown in them" (Mark 4:15).

4. **He constantly accuses us before God**. We are incriminated by Satan 24 hours a day, seven days a week. Revelation 12:10 reads, "For the accuser of our brethren has been thrown down, he who accuses them before our God day and night."

5. **He wants to devour us**. We must be alert at all times because Satan is looking for someone to swallow up and destroy. 1 Peter 5:8 reads, "Be of sober spirit, be on the alert. Your adversary, the devil, prowls around like a roaring lion, seeking someone to devour."

6. **He tries to hinder us**. Satan is trying to stop us from doing what God wants us to do. 1 Thessalonians 2:18 reads, "For we wanted to come to you--I, Paul, more than once-- and yet Satan hindered us."

7. **He works hard at deceiving us**. Satan pretends to be someone he is not to trick us into trusting him.

2 Corinthians 11:14 reads, "No wonder, for even Satan disguises himself as an angel of light."

8. **He desires to lead us astray**. Satan wants us to follow him, so he tries to keep our focus off of Jesus. 2 Corinthians 11:3 reads, "But I am afraid that, as the serpent deceived Eve by his craftiness, your minds will be led astray from the simplicity and purity of devotion to Christ."

What should we do when Satan attacks us? James gives us a simple strategy: "Submit therefore to God. Resist the devil and he will flee from you" (James 4:7).

STOP letting Satan run you down. It's time for you to run him away. How do we make Satan run? Submit to God (through faith) and resist Satan. Then Satan will run. Submitting and resisting is exactly what Jesus did when Satan attacked him.

The Bible reads, "Then Jesus was led up by the Spirit into the wilderness to be tempted by the devil. And after He had fasted forty days and forty nights, He then became hungry. And the tempter came and said to Him, "If You are the Son of God, command that these stones become bread." But He answered and said, "It is written, 'MAN SHALL NOT LIVE ON BREAD ALONE, BUT ON EVERY WORD THAT PROCEEDS OUT OF THE MOUTH OF GOD.'" Then the devil took Him into the holy city and had Him stand on the pinnacle of the temple, and said to Him, "If You are the Son of God, throw Yourself down; for it is written, 'HE WILL COMMAND HIS ANGELS CONCERNING YOU'; and 'ON their HANDS THEY WILL BEAR YOU UP, SO THAT YOU WILL NOT STRIKE YOUR FOOT AGAINST A STONE.'" Jesus said to him, "On the other hand, it is written, 'YOU SHALL NOT PUT THE LORD YOUR GOD TO THE TEST.'" Again, the devil took Him to a very high mountain and showed Him all the kingdoms of the world and their glory; and he said to Him, "All these things I will give You, if You fall down and worship me." Then Jesus said to him, "Go, Satan! For it is written, 'YOU SHALL WORSHIP THE LORD YOUR GOD, AND SERVE HIM ONLY.'" Then the devil left Him; and behold, angels came and began to minister to Him (Matthew 4:1-11).

Satan attacked Jesus three times with various temptations. How did Jesus fight the devil's temptations? Jesus submitted to God and resisted

Satan with every temptation. Jesus used his faith! He resisted by putting His *hope* and *confidence* in God and His word (the Bible). Each time Satan tempted Jesus, he fought that temptation with the word of God.

After Jesus submitted to God and resisted Satan's temptation, the devil left Jesus alone. Jesus made Satan run! When we submit to God (through faith) and resist temptation, Satan runs the other way!

When Satan tempts you with lust, make him run with the Job 31:1, "I made a covenant with my eyes not to look with lust at a young woman." If Satan tempts you to overeat or abuse alcohol and drugs, make him run with 1 Corinthians 6:19, "My body is the temple of the Holy Spirit."

When Satan tempts you to gossip, make him run with Ephesians 4:29, "No unwholesome word proceed from my mouth, but only such a word as is good for edification according to the need of the moment, so that it will give grace to those who hear." God's word is your weapon to defeat Satan.

Now that we know how to make Satan run through our faith, let's focus on our not so obvious enemy. I believe our other enemy is the person that attacks us and attempts to keep us from obeying God. This enemy can be your husband, wife, son, daughter, father, mother, brother, sister, aunt, uncle, niece, nephew, cousin, neighbor, employer, employee, co-worker, friend, BFF, church member, and even your pastor.

Satan uses this person to attack you and keep you from walking with God. In order to defeat this enemy we must realize that "our struggle is not against flesh and blood, but against the rulers, against the powers, against the world forces of this darkness, against the spiritual forces of wickedness in the heavenly places" (Ephesians 6:12). We should fight spirits not people.

When this enemy attacks you, fight Satan instead of fighting the person. You must overcome the spirit within them. You must defeat Satan. Once again, Jesus shows us how to do it. Lets turn to Matthew's Gospel to see what Jesus did.

"Now when Jesus came into the district of Caesarea Philippi, He was asking His disciples, "Who do people say that the Son of Man is?" And they said, "Some say John the Baptist; and others, Elijah; but still others, Jeremiah, or one of the prophets." He said to them, "But who do you say that I am?" Simon Peter answered, "You are the Christ, the Son of the living God" (Matthew 16:13-16).

Did you notice what Peter did? First, Peter acknowledged Jesus' deity. Peter recognized Jesus as "the Christ, the Son of the Living God."

Before the other disciples could congratulate Peter on getting the answer right, Jesus said, "Blessed are you, Simon Barjona, because flesh and blood did not reveal this to you, but My Father who is in heaven" (Matthew 16:17).

The Spirit of God revealed Jesus' true identity to Peter. Peter saw Jesus as more than a preacher, teacher, prophet, or healer. He saw Jesus as the Messiah, the Chosen One of God. Peter recognized the anointing of God in the life of Jesus. Moments later, after Peter acknowledged Jesus, he attacked Jesus.

"From that time Jesus began to show His disciples that He must go to Jerusalem, and suffer many things from the elders and chief priests and scribes, and be killed, and be raised up on the third day. Peter took Him aside and began to rebuke Him, saying, "God forbid it, Lord! This shall never happen to You." But He turned and said to Peter, "Get behind Me, Satan! You are a stumbling block to Me; for you are not setting your mind on God's interests, but man's" (Matthew 16:21-23).

Jesus recognized Satan. He called out the devil and rebuked Him. The devil was using Peter, a friend of Jesus to hinder Christ from achieving his destiny. Satan's trick did not work. Jesus recognized Satan's game. He called out the devil and rebuked him.

Jesus would have been distracted from His destiny if he listened to Peter. Satan tried to defeat Jesus through a disciple. However, Jesus did not let anyone keep him from obeying God, not even his disciples. Jesus fulfilled his destiny on the cross. He suffered and died on Calvary. He was raised from the dead by the power of God, which was the ultimate victory over Satan.

So who is your enemy? Your enemy is anyone that tries to keep you from obeying God. This means any of our family, friends, co-workers, or church members can be our enemy. The person attempting to stop you from achieving your God-given destiny is your enemy. Do you have a dream-killer in your life. That person is the enemy. Do you have a joy-stealer in your life. That person is the enemy.
Do you have a hope-destroyer in your life? That person is your enemy. No matter their relationship to you, they are your enemy (for the moment) if they are trying to kill, steal, and your destroy you.

Jesus said, "the thief comes to kill, steal, and destroy." The thief in your life is your enemy.

How should we fight this enemy? First, we must recognize the person is not the enemy. Satan and his demonic forces are the true enemy. Second, we must resist temptation because when Satan will flee when we resist him. Third, we must rebuke the demonic influence in that person. If someone discourages you from moving toward your destiny, speak the words of Jesus: "get behind me Satan." If a person is tempting to you to sin, just say, "get behind me Satan." Our dreams are killed. Our joy is stolen. Our hope is destroyed because we cannot recognize our enemy, resist temptation, and rebuke the enemy. Anyone trying to get you to disobey God, or distracting you from your destiny is an enemy. Recognize your enemy so you can resist temptation and rebuke your enemy. Don't be defeated! Use your FAITH to submit and resist! When you submit and resist (through faith) your enemy will run away!!

Think About It!

1. Who are our enemies?

2. How does Satan try to defeat us?

3. How does Satan use people to attack us?

4. What did Jesus do when Satan attacked him?

5. How do we defeat Satan and those he uses to attack us?

3

KNOW JESUS

Ok, let's summarize what we have discovered so far: 1) Faith gives us victory and 2) Faith helps us overcome our enemies. Our enemies are Satan and those that try to keep us from obeying God.

This leads to another key for spiritual victory. In whom do we put our faith? Let's read verse 1 John 5:5 for the third key. "Who is the one who overcomes the world, but he who believes that Jesus is the Son of God?" Jesus is the one in whom we should place our faith.

Did you notice why we should put our faith in Jesus? We win the battle against the world, when we believe in Jesus. We overcome Satan and all is evil schemes through faith in Jesus Christ.

Satan does not want you to win. Do you remember 1 Peter 5:8? "Your adversary, the devil, prowls around like a roaring lion, seeking someone to devour." Satan does not want you to be an overcomer. He does not want you to have the victory. He tries to keep you from obeying God and knowing the truth. He wants you to lose by any means necessary.

Satan does not fight fair. He will try to use whatever and whoever to defeat you. Satan tries to use your family, friends, finances, failures, and health to conquer you! Do not be discouraged or dismayed! If you have faith in Jesus, you are a winner! You are an overcomer! You have the victory!

You will conquer the devil, his demons, devises, and all of his deception through faith in Jesus. Put your faith in Jesus because with Jesus you win the battle.

Who is Jesus? According to verse 5, "Jesus is the Son of God." What does "Son of God" mean? In this verse the phrase "Son of God" has two meanings. First, "Son of God" means that there is a unique relationship between Jesus and God. The first reference is the baptism of Jesus.[1]

"After being baptized, Jesus came up immediately from the water; and behold, the heavens were opened, and he saw the Spirit of God descending as a dove and lighting on Him, and behold, a voice out of the heavens said, "This is My beloved Son, in whom I am well-pleased" (Matthew 3:16-17).

Now let's read about what happened when Jesus was on a mountain with some of His disciples.

"Six days later Jesus took with Him Peter and James and John his brother, and led them up on a high mountain by themselves. And He was transfigured before them; and His face shone like the sun, and His garments became as white as light.

And behold, Moses and Elijah appeared to them, talking with Him. Peter said to Jesus, "Lord, it is good for us to be here; if You wish, I will make three tabernacles here, one for You, and one for Moses, and one for Elijah."

While he was still speaking, a bright cloud overshadowed them, and behold, a voice out of the cloud said, "This is My beloved Son, with whom I am well-pleased; listen to Him!" (Matthew 17:1-6).

Did you notice what God said about Jesus? Both times God said, "This is My beloved Son, with whom I am well-pleased." God also said, "Listen to Him." God wanted people to know He was well-pleased with His beloved Son (Jesus), and God commanded people to listen to Jesus.

The Apostle Paul also called Jesus God's beloved son. Colossians 1:13 reads, "for He rescued us from the domain of darkness, and transferred us to the kingdom of His *beloved Son*."

What does beloved mean? It means their Father-Son relationship is one of love. John 3:35 reads, "The Father loves the Son and has given all things into His hand." Beloved means Jesus is the embodiment of God's love. He is the revelation of God. Their Father-Son relationship existed before creation. There is no one like Jesus because he is unique and one of a kind.

All Christians have a relationship with God. He is our Father and we are His children. However, we do not have the same *unique* relationship with God that Jesus has with God because Jesus is the beloved son. According to Dr. John Piper, "when we call Jesus the Son of God, we should have in our minds the truth that he is God and that there is a relationship of infinite love between God the Father and God the Son that is different from all other loves."[2] So the first meaning for Son of God refers to the unique relationship with God and Jesus.

What is the second meaning for the phrase Son of God? The phrase Son of God also means that **Jesus is God**. Jesus is more than an angel. He is more than a man. Jesus is fully God and fully man. The Bible affirms this several times. John 1:1 reads, "In the beginning was the Word, and the Word was with God, and the Word was God."

The Word (logos) is the embodiment (message) of the invisible God. Jesus Christ was present when time began in Genesis chapter 1. He was with God, and he was God. So the Word is distinct from God, yet he is one with God. Oneness indicates he was not separate from God. It means to be in one accord. So the Word and God are not two but one. If he was with God, then he is aware of all that God did. Since he is one with God, he did everything God did.

John 10:30 reads "I and the Father are one." Jesus was saying that he and the Father are one in purpose and will.[3]

Everything Jesus did while on earth, he did in one accord with God the Father. They have unity of purpose. Jesus' will is the same as the Father's will.

Colossians 2:9 reads, "For in Him all the fullness of Deity dwells in bodily form." Some religions teach that Jesus was an angel or a man. This verse affirms that Jesus is 100 percent God and 100 percent man. The fullness of God lives in Jesus in bodily form. We have the truth of God through Jesus Christ.[4]

John wrote his gospel so that people might "believe that Jesus is the Christ, the Son of God" (John 20:31). Do you believe that Jesus Christ is the Son of God? Consider these three truths:

1. 1 John 5:12 reads, "He who has the Son has the life; he who does not have the Son of God does not have the life."
2. 1 John 2:23 reads, "Whoever denies the Son does not have the Father; the one who confesses the Son has the Father also."

3. Galatians 2:20 reads, "the *life* which I now live in the flesh I live by faith in the Son of God, who loved me and gave Himself up for me."

As the Son of God, **Jesus is God**. Therefore, he has the same attributes as God. Whatever is true of God is also true of Jesus Christ.

- Jesus is all-knowing. John 2:24-25, But Jesus, on His part, was not entrusting Himself to them, for He knew all men, and because He did not need anyone to testify concerning man, for He Himself knew what was in man.

- Jesus is all-powerful, "All authority has been given to Me in heaven and on earth." Matthew 28:18.

- Jesus reveals "grace and truth." John 1:17.

- Jesus is holy. "For we do not have a high priest who cannot sympathize with our weaknesses, but One who has been tempted

in all things as we are, yet without sin."
(Hebrews 4:15)

- Jesus is unchanging. "Jesus Christ *is* the same yesterday and today and forever." Hebrews 13:8.

- Jesus is wise. "But by His doing you are in Christ Jesus, who became to us wisdom from God, and righteousness and sanctification, and redemption." 1 Corinthians 1:30.

- Jesus is compassionate. Seeing the people, He felt compassion for them, because they were distressed and dispirited like sheep without a shepherd. Matthew 9:36.

- Jesus is patient. "Yet for this reason I found mercy, so that in me as the foremost, Jesus Christ might demonstrate His perfect patience as an example for those who would believe in Him for eternal life."- 1 Timothy 1:16.

Jesus is God. When I read the gospels, I see the deity of Jesus on display. He has the power to create without a blueprint. He has the power to predict and control the weather without Doppler radar. Jesus can heal the sick without medical treatment. He can make the paralyzed walk without rehab. He can raise the dead back to life without CPR. Jesus can do all things. Jesus is God! So put your faith in Jesus because He is the Son of God.

We will be overcomers when we put our faith in Jesus!!

How would our families change if we put our faith in Jesus? Husbands would love their wives as Christ loved the church. Wives would submit to their husbands as unto the Lord. Children would obey their parents in all things (Colossians 3:18-21)!

How would our communities look different if our churches were full of overcomers? Our churches would turn their communities upside down.

We would proclaim the Gospel to the poor. We would proclaim freedom for prisoners. There would be recovery of sight for the spiritually blind. And the oppressed would be set free. People would begin to live in the favor and grace of God (Luke 4:18-19).

What if our youth and children became overcomers? Our children would be bold instead of being bullied. Our youth would excel instead of being expelled from school. Our youth would focus on graduation instead of joining gangs. Our youth would be serious about school instead of being silly in school. They would live the truth instead of living a lie. They would talk more about Jesus instead of telling instead of telling jokes. They would live in VICTORY! Do you want to live a life of victory? Have faith in Jesus! When we put our faith in Jesus we become overcomers. He is our Champion! When we put our faith in Jesus, we have victory! **"Thanks be to God, who gives us the victory through our Lord Jesus Christ"** (1 Corinthians 15:57).

Think About It!

1. In whom should we put our faith?

2. Why should we put our faith in Jesus?

3. What is the first meaning for the Son of God?

4. What is the second meaning for the Son of God?

5. Why do you believe that Jesus is God?

CONCLUSION

So let's summarize what we have discovered about spiritual victory:

1. Faith gives us victory.
2. Faith helps us overcome our enemies: Satan and those keeping us from obeying God.
3. We must put our faith in Jesus for victory because He is the Son of God.

Are you an overcomer? Do you have the victory? Christians are overcomers! With faith in Jesus Christ, the Son of God, victory is inevitable! Can you envision how our lives would change if we put our faith in Jesus for victory?

- We would have assurance not anxiety!
- We would see our blessings and stop being bitter!
- We would conquer instead of living in conflict!

- We would dominate instead of being defeated.

- We would be energized for life not exhausted from life's troubles.

- We would feel God's favor instead of feeling failure!

- We would be victorious not victims!

Spiritual Victory is yours. Seize victory today. Victory is mine, victory is mine, victory today is mine. I told Satan, get thee behind. Victory today is mine.

My Testimony:

How I Became I Christian

I did not have relationship with God before I became a Christian. I was committed to going to church, but I was not committed to God. I would lie, steal, and disobey my parents.

My relationship with God began one evening when watching Dr. Charles F. Stanley on In Touch. He proclaimed the gospel at the end of his sermon. I realized four things after hearing the gospel: 1) I was a sinner; 2) the wages of sin is death; 3) I needed a Savior; 4) Jesus Christ (the Savior) died for my sins and rose from the dead. So that evening I repented of my sins, and I believed in Christ as my Savior. I asked God to forgive me for my sins, and I surrendered my life to Him.

When I became a Christian, I felt like a new person. The Bible says, " Therefore if any man be in Christ, he is a new creature: old things are passed away; behold, new things have come" (2 Corinthians 5:17). My whole life changed. I committed my life to Christ and His Church. I desired God and godly things. I had more than religion; I had a relationship with God. I read the Bible everyday and communicated with God through prayer and worship. I was not satisfied with being good. I wanted to be like Jesus Christ; I wanted to be holy. That's my testimony: the story of how I became a Christian.

Do you want to become a Christian? It is simple! Turn away from your sins and trust in Jesus to save you from your sins!

APPENDIX

20 Names of Satan

1. The prince of the power of the air (Ephesians 2:2)
2. The god of this age (2 Corinthians 4:4)
3. The king of death (Hebrews 2:14)
4. The prince of this world (John 12:31)
5. The ruler of darkness (Ephesians 6:12)
6. Leviathan—one who dwells in sea of humanity (Isaiah 27:1)
7. Lucifer-light-bearer, shining one (Isaiah 14:12)
8. The dragon (Revelation 12:7)
9. The deceiver (Revelation 20:10)
10. Apollyon—destroyer (Revelation 9:11)
11. Beelzebub—prince of demons (Matthew 12:24)
12. Belial—ruthlessness (2 Corinthians 6:15)
13. The evil one (Matthew 13:38)
14. The tempter (1 Thessalonians 3:5)
15. The accuser of the brethren (Revelation 12:10)

16. An angel of light (2 Corinthians 11:14-15)

17. A liar (John 8:44, Genesis 3:4-5)

18. A murderer (John 8:44)

19. The enemy (Matthew 13:39)

20. A roaring lion (1 Peter 5:8)[8]

NOTES

Chapter 1: Know the Secret
1. John MacArthur, *MacArthur Study Bible*, (Nashville: Thomas Nelson, 2006), 1943.

Chapter 2: Know Your Enemies
1. Merrill F. Unger, *Evangelical dictionary of theology*, ed. Walter A. Elwell (Grand Rapids, MI: Baker Academic, a division of Baker Publishing Group, 2001), 1054.
2. Joel R. Beeke, *Fighting Satan: knowing his weaknesses, strategies, and defeat* (Grand Rapids, MI: Reformation Heritage Books, 2015), 77-86.

Chapter 3: Know Jesus
1. John MacArthur, 1943.
2. John Piper, "Jesus Is the Christ the Son of God." Desiring God, 6 Oct. 1991, www.desiringgod.org/messages/jesus-is-the-christ-the-son-of-god; accessed, Sept. 21, 2017.
3. Gerald L. Borchert, *John 1–11*, vol. 25A, The New American Commentary (Nashville: Broadman & Holman Publishers, 1996), 341.
4. Richard R. Melick, *Philippians, Colossians, Philemon*, vol. 32, The New American Commentary (Nashville: Broadman & Holman Publishers, 1991), 254–255.

Appendix B: 20 Names of Satan
1. H.L. Willmington, *Willmington's Book of Bible Lists* (Wheaton, IL: Tyndale, 1987), 301–302.

ACKNOWLEDGEMENTS

Thank you to God for saving me, so I can serve him. Thank you to my family for always inspiring and encouraging me. This book project was inspired from a sermon that I preached to Greater Shiloh Missionary Baptist Church of Headland, AL during for a youth revival. Thank you to Pastor Delvick McKay and Greater Shiloh Missionary Baptist Church for supporting my ministry. Thank you to Macedonia Missionary Baptist Church for the opportunity to expand my ministry beyond the pulpit. Thank you to my wife, Catesha. I could not have finished this project without you. Thank you to the Jesse Nelson ministry team.

FROM THE AUTHOR…

Thanks for reading Spiritual Victory. I hope this book gave you inspiration and insight for living in victory and growing in Christ. Although the book is *short*, I believe that the application of the simple truths within these pages will make a dynamic difference in your life.

Be Blessed, Jesse Nelson

For seminars, speaking, bulk copies of books, publishing, or general questions call 334.202.1821

**P.O. Box 62
Panama City, FL 32402**

or visit our website:
www.jessenelson.org

or Facebook:
Jesse Nelson Ministries

Other books published by Jesse Nelson Ministries:
The Authenticity of Christianity
My Prayer Book
Count It All Joy: A Devotional Workbook for James

ABOUT THE AUTHOR…

Jesse L. Nelson is the founder of Jesse Nelson Ministries and senior pastor of Macedonia Missionary Baptist Church of Panama City, FL. He is a dynamic speaker and author of *The Authenticity of Christianity, My Prayer Book*, and *Count It All Joy: A Devotional Workbook for James*. Jesse enjoys writing for his blog, *Theology, Discipleship & Ministry*. He is an adjunct professor at the Baptist College of Florida in Graceville, FL and completed studies at Selma University, New Orleans Baptist Theological Seminary, Alabama State University, Auburn University, and Oxford University. He serves as a mentor to pastors and a missionary to Haiti. He is happily married (Catesha) with two children (Jacey and Carey).

www.ingramcontent.com/pod-product-compliance
Lightning Source LLC
Chambersburg PA
CBHW071733020426
42331CB00008B/2004